Letts

You think *you* have a long journey to school? Meet the Alien Club, a group of jolly aliens from the planet Dunk. They all entered a competition and won first prize – to go to school on planet Earth, six thousand light years away! Lucky their space-mobile runs on recycled rubbish and can travel a hundred light years in a heartbeat!

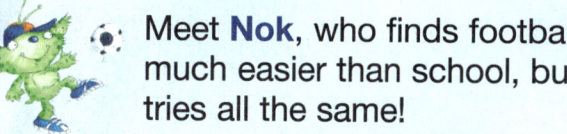 Meet **Nok**, who finds football much easier than school, but tries all the same!

Twinx, who loves ribbons, dancing and her toy friend Mini T.

Bouncing **Pogo**, who just can't stand still!

 Pogo's pet dog, the rather less lively **Zen**, who won't get out of bed for less than a Z cookie or two.

 **Zara P**, zip zip zipping around on her scooter and making notes on everything she sees.

 And **Zing**, who loves his music most of all, but thinks school is pretty cool too!

Now the Alien Club want to pass on everything they have learnt to you. All you have to do is work your way through these tests and not only will you be the cleverest Earthling around, you'll become a member of the Alien Club too! Out of this world!!!

English 7–8

Test 1	Adding **ing**	Test 17	Antonyms
Test 2	**le** endings	Test 18	Adjectives
Test 3	The alphabet	Test 19	Homonyms
Test 4	Synonyms	Test 20	Pronouns
Test 5	Handwriting	Test 21	Conjunctions
Test 6	Verbs	Test 22	Commas
Test 7	Prefixes	Test 23	Nouns
Test 8	Verb tenses	Test 24	Fact and fiction
Test 9	Speech marks	Test 25	Instructions
Test 10	**er** and **est**	Test 26	Words within words
Test 11	Writing dialogue	Test 27	Setting
Test 12	Silent letters	Test 28	Finding information
Test 13	Compound words		
Test 14	Suffixes **ly** and **ful**	Page 30	Answers
Test 15	Contracting words	Page 32	Certificate
Test 16	Prefixes **mis** and **non**		

Alison Head

TEST 1: Adding ing

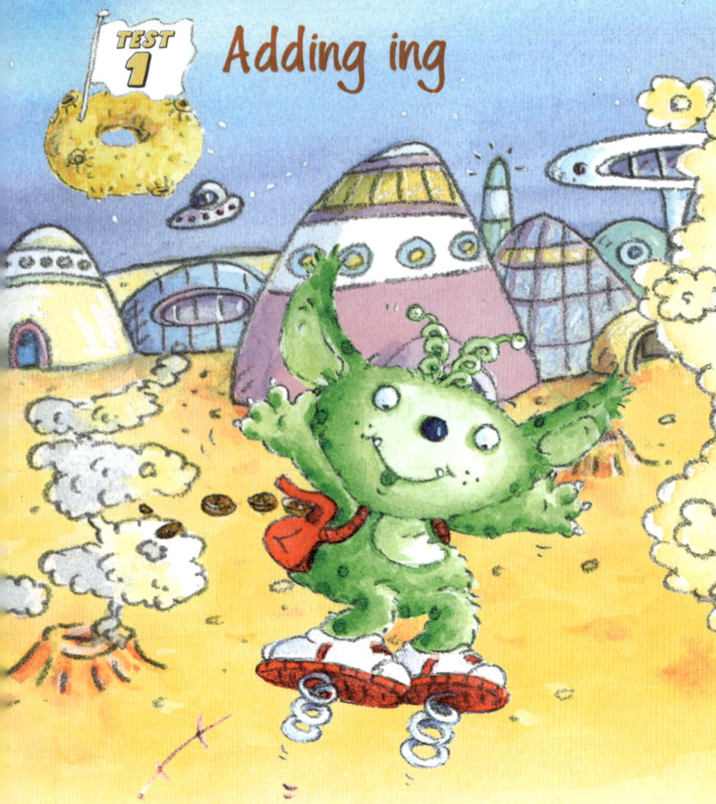

Boing, boing, boing! I'm Pogo and I'm always bounc**ing** about! Adding **ing** to a verb like 'bounce' tells people something is happening right now. If the verb ends in **e**, you must take the **e** off first.

bounc**e**   bounc**ing**

If the verb has a short vowel sound before the final letter, you double that last letter.

ho**p**   ho**pp**ing

Try these word sums. Don't forget the spelling rules for adding ing!

1. run + ing = _____
2. make + ing = _____
3. rain + ing = _____
4. tap + ing = _____
5. play + ing = _____
6. go + ing = _____
7. swim + ing = _____
8. take + ing = _____
9. hope + ing = _____
10. dance + ing = _____
11. say + ing = _____
12. win + ing = _____

Put a spring in your step! Have a springy sticker for your certificate at the back of the book.

Colour in your score.

TEST 2: le endings

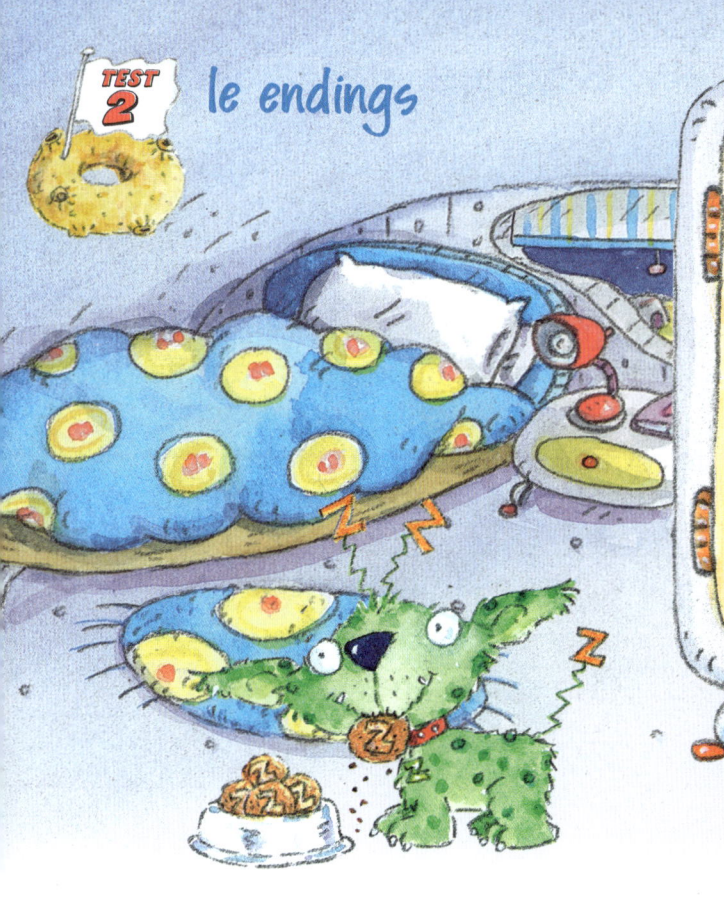

Hello, I'm Zen, Pogo's faithful friend. I prefer sleeping and eating to bouncing. These Z cookies taste great, but they always crumb**le** everywhere, making a huge mudd**le**! Lots of words end in **le**, but the spelling patterns **al** and **el** sound the same, so you need to remember which ending to use.

I might need another Z cookie for this one!

Circle the correctly spelt word in each pair.

1. appel / apple
2. bottle / bottel
3. pettle / petal
4. angel / angal
5. littel / little
6. parcel / parcle
7. tabel / table
8. modle / model
9. metal / metel
10. pedal / pedel
11. medal / medel
12. labal / label

Colour in your score.

Good work! Have a Z cookie sticker for your certificate at the back of the book.

TEST 3 The alphabet

Hi, I'm Nok and I'm football crazy! Scoring a goal is tricky, but finding words in the dictionary is easy if you know roughly where each letter appears in the **alphabet**. For example, **c** is near the start of the alphabet, so words beginning with **c** will be near the front of the dictionary.

He shoots, he scores!

Imagine this goal is the alphabet, then write roughly where you think each of these letters belongs.

1 M
2 X
3 E
4 N
5 T
6 B
7 H
8 O
9 S
10 F
11 L
12 Q

Goal! Have a football sticker for your certificate.

Colour in your score.

TEST 4 Synonyms

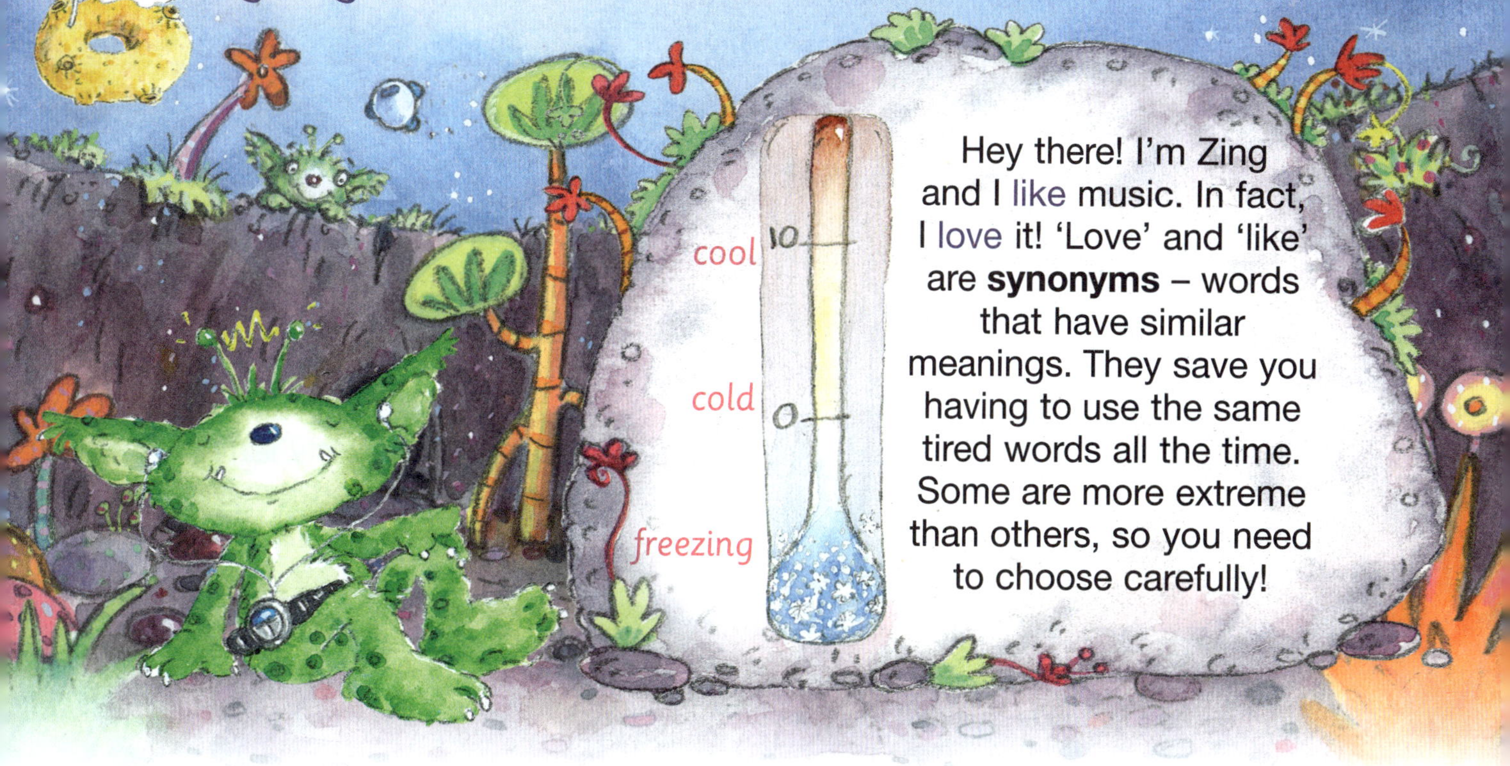

Hey there! I'm Zing and I like music. In fact, I love it! 'Love' and 'like' are **synonyms** – words that have similar meanings. They save you having to use the same tired words all the time. Some are more extreme than others, so you need to choose carefully!

cool
cold
freezing

Join up each of these words with a more extreme synonym from the jukebox.

ancient
fascinating
scorching
miserable
hilarious
smashed
delighted
gigantic
exhausted
dazzling
starving
tiny

1 hot
2 funny
3 tired
4 sad
5 large
6 pleased

7 bright
8 hungry
9 small
10 interesting
11 broken
12 old

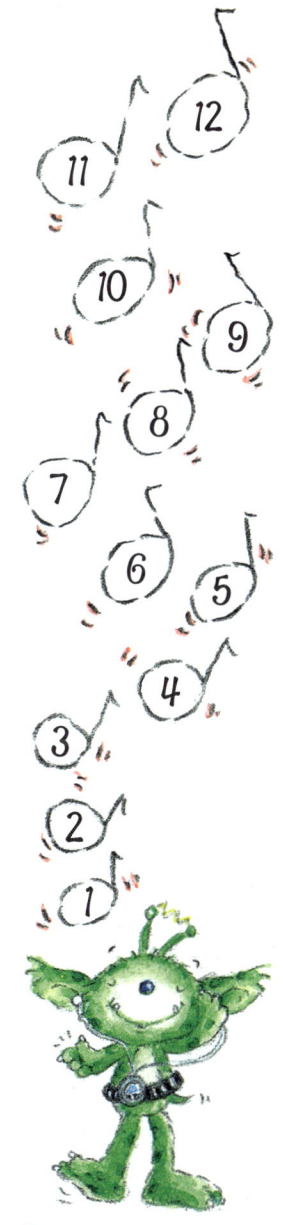

Easy! Have a musical sticker for your certificate.

Colour in your score.

TEST 5 Handwriting

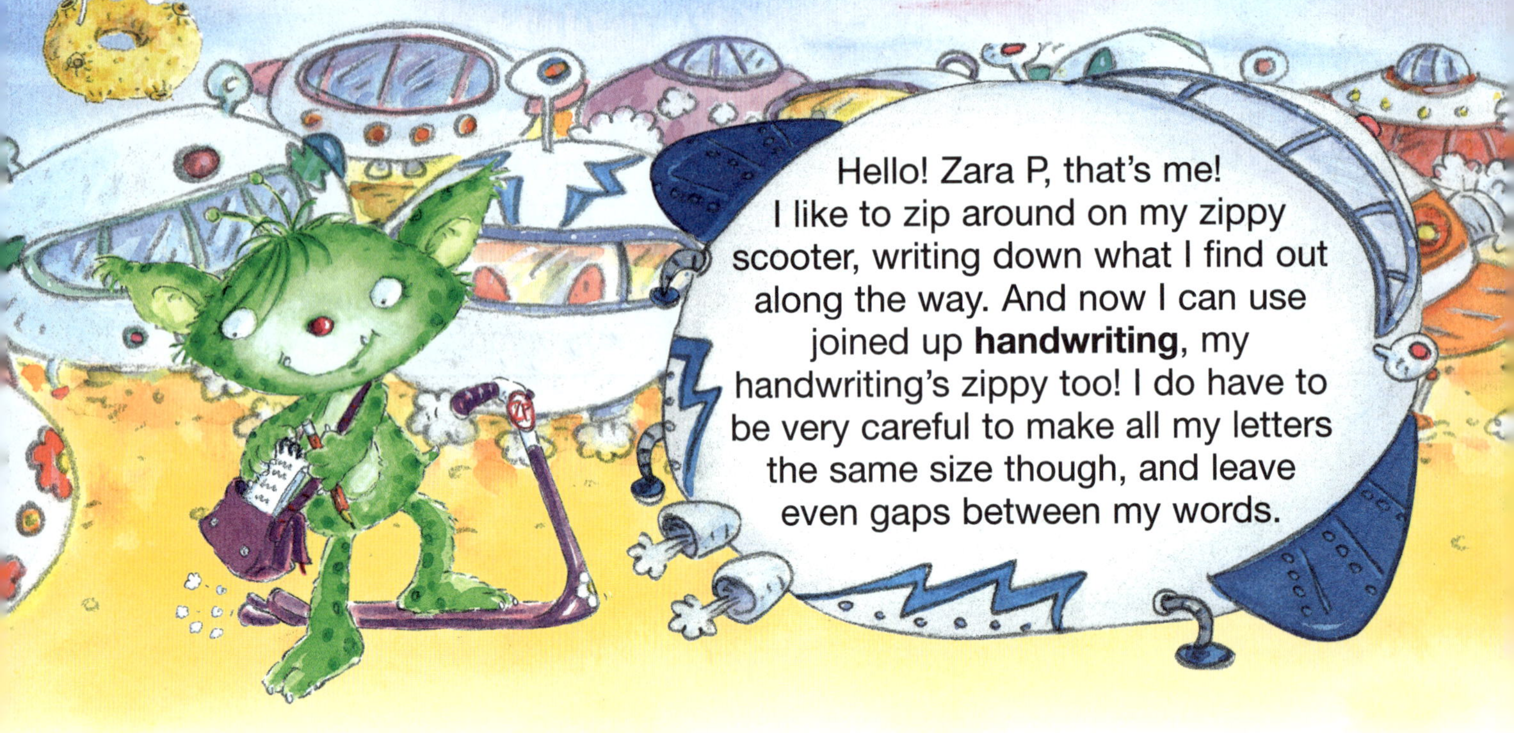
Hello! Zara P, that's me!
I like to zip around on my zippy scooter, writing down what I find out along the way. And now I can use joined up **handwriting**, my handwriting's zippy too! I do have to be very careful to make all my letters the same size though, and leave even gaps between my words.

Write out these phrases again, using joined up writing.

1 paint pot ____________________

2 silver star ____________________

3 funny face ____________________

4 loud sound ____________________

5 grape vine ____________________

6 two twins ____________________

7 roundabout ____________________

8 full stop ____________________

9 table mat ____________________

10 fairground ____________________

11 white cloud ____________________

12 wild witch ____________________

12
11
10
9
8
7
6
5
4
3
2
1

Colour in your score.

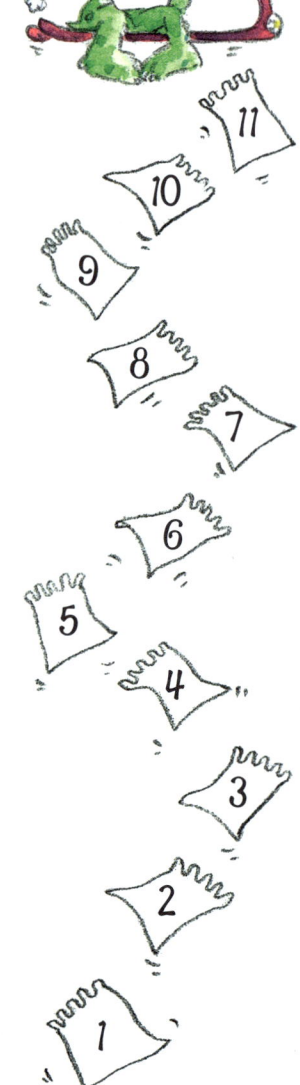

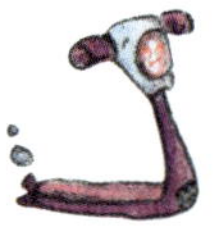

You're zippy! Have a scooter sticker.

TEST 6 Verbs

Look at my pal Pogo go! **Bounce**, **hop** and **spring** are all **verbs** you could use to describe what he's doing. He spends so long hopping about, it's good to have a few different verbs to choose from! Choosing the right verb can also tell us exactly how someone does something.

Pogo **hops**   Pogo **bounds**

Draw lines to match up pairs of verbs with similar meanings.

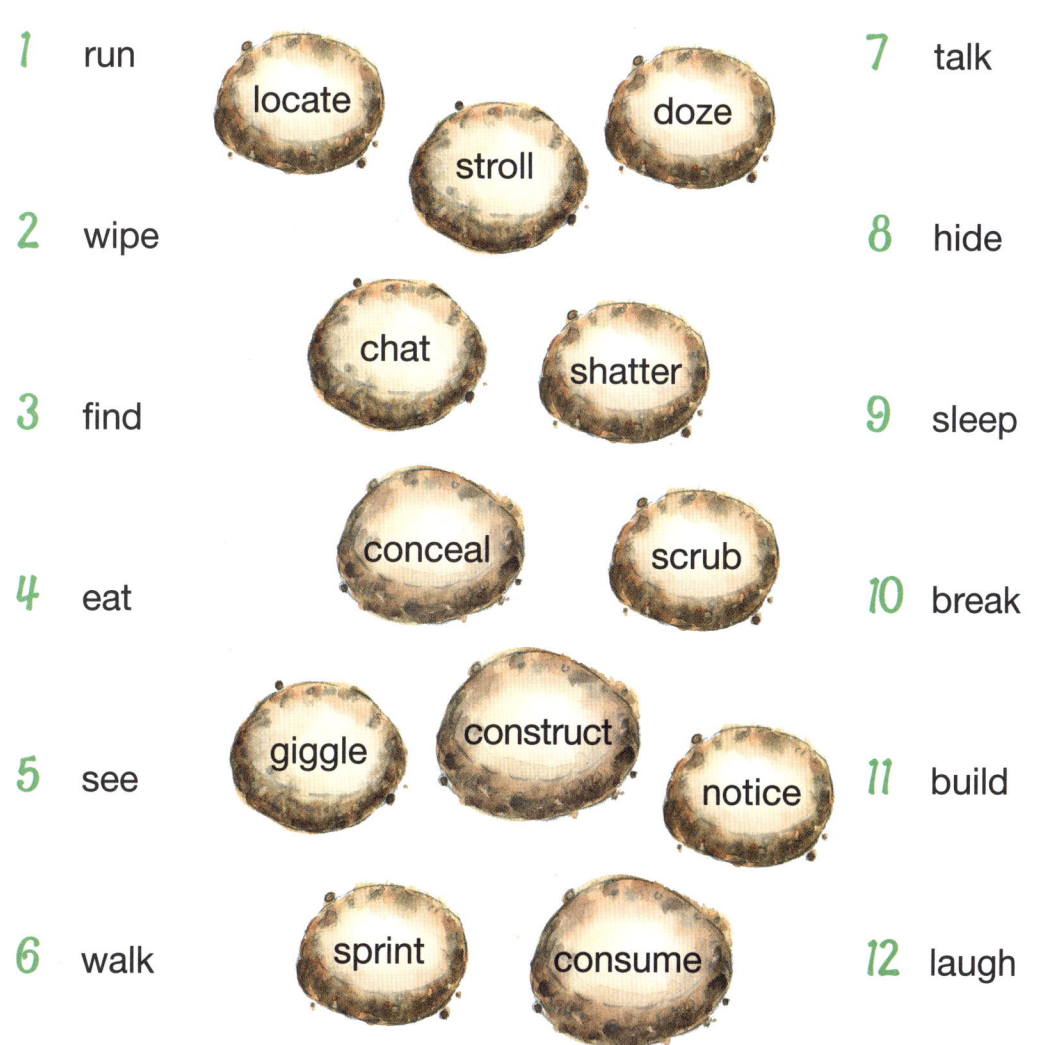

1 run
2 wipe
3 find
4 eat
5 see
6 walk

locate
stroll
doze
chat
shatter
conceal
scrub
giggle
construct
notice
sprint
consume

7 talk
8 hide
9 sleep
10 break
11 build
12 laugh

 Good work! Have a Z cookie sticker.

Colour in your score.

Test 7 Prefixes

New words are just a bounce away if you know how to use **prefixes**. They are groups of letters you can add to the start of some words to alter their meaning. Different prefixes have different meanings.

un and **dis** usually mean 'not'
unreal, **dis**obey

pre means 'before' **pre**view

re means 'again' **re**turn

Write a definition of these words, for example, unhappy = not happy

1. undone _____
2. preschool _____
3. disappear _____
4. unusual _____
5. disapprove _____
6. displeased _____
7. undressed _____
8. repaint _____
9. precooked _____
10. rewrite _____
11. reform _____
12. prepaid _____

Put a spring in your step! Have a springy sticker.

Colour in your score.

Verb tenses

Hello, I'm Twinx and this is my toy friend Mini T. We like ribbons and pretty dresses and most of all – dancing! Did you know, **dance** is a **verb**, and the **tense** of a verb tells us whether something is happening, or happened in the past.

I dance now.   I danced yesterday.

Hurray! Come on, Mini T, let's dance right now!

Fill in the missing present and past tense verbs on the chart.

	Present	Past
1	walk	_____
2	_____	bought
3	save	_____
4	tip	_____
5	_____	hid
6	_____	wrote
7	hurry	_____
8	swim	_____
9	_____	ran
10	grow	_____
11	_____	saw
12	_____	knew

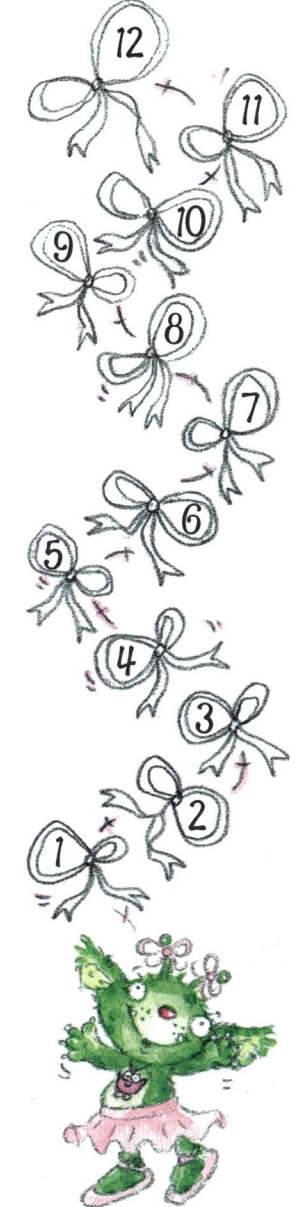

Hurray! Have a Mini T sticker.

Colour in your score.

Speech marks

Zip, zip, zip!
Speech marks go at the start and end of a passage of speech, to show readers that someone is speaking. I wish it was as easy to find a pen in my bag!

'I've lost my pen,' complained Zara P.

Pogo said, 'Borrow mine.'

Can you see the speech mark always goes after the comma?

Add the speech marks to these sentences. Use the examples above to help you.

1. I'm playing football later, said Nok.
2. Zing said, This music is so cool.
3. Can I have a Z cookie? asked Zen.
4. Zara P said, Do you like my scooter?
5. Twinx said, I'm dancing with Mini T.
6. Pogo said, Just bouncing around!
7. Nok shouted, Did you see that goal?
8. Zen mumbled, I'm sleepy.
9. Look at my new music player, said Zing.
10. Here comes the space-mobile, said Zara P.
11. Pogo said, Let's hop over to the crater field.
12. Twinx asked, Do you like my dance?

You're zippy! Have a scooter sticker.

Colour in your score.

Test 10 — er and est

I can run fast**er** than anyone on Dunk, which makes me the fast**est**! **Er** and **est** are suffixes that can make adjectives tell us even more about the person or thing they are describing.

big   bigg**er**   bigg**est**

Sometimes the spelling of the root word has to change before you add **er** or **est**.

He shoots, he scores!

Complete these words sums. Remember to think about whether you need to change the spelling of the root word.

1 tall + est = _____

2 _____ + er = hungrier

3 short + er = _____

4 close + est = _____

5 _____ + er = darker

6 pretty + est = _____

7 _____ + er = happier

8 _____ + er = later

9 safe + est = _____

10 _____ + est = hottest

11 fit + er = _____

12 old + er = _____

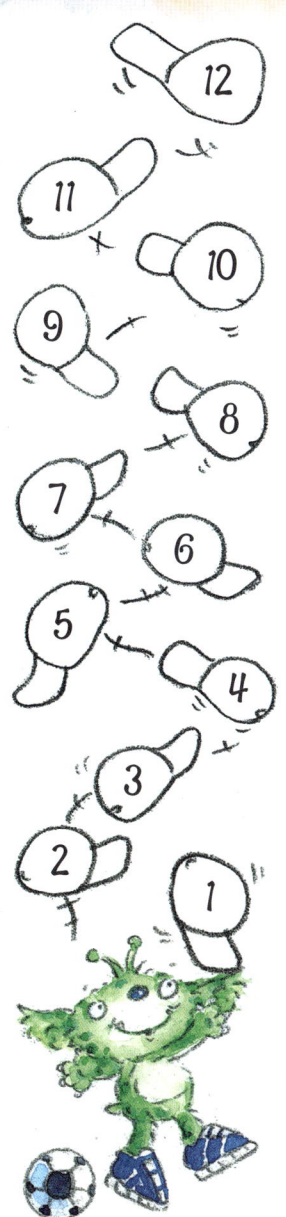

Goal! Have a football sticker.

Colour in your score.

Test 11: Writing dialogue

I know who sings all my favourite songs. When I'm reading though, I have to rely on the writer to tell me who is saying what.

'Time to go,' **said** Pogo.

A writer can also say more about what is being said, like whether it's a question, or an exclamation, for example.

'Where's Twinx**?**' **asked** Nok.
'Over here**!**' **shouted** Twinx.

Circle the best word to complete each sentence.

1. 'That was a foul!' _____ Nok. | asked shouted
2. 'I fancy a nap,' _____ Zen. | yawned giggled
3. 'Have you seen Mini T?' _____ Twinx. | asked whispered
4. Nok _____, 'Yes, she's over there.' | replied questioned
5. 'Why did you turn my music off?' _____ Zing, angrily. | demanded answered
6. 'It was too loud,' _____ Zara P. | questioned explained
7. 'Watch out, here I come!' _____ Pogo. | insisted warned
8. 'Slow down before you break something,' _____ Zen. | advised questioned
9. Zara P _____, 'The space-mobile is late today.' | argued observed
10. Twinx _____, 'I've lost one of my ribbons.' | grumbled asked
11. 'Do you fancy a Z cookie?' _____ Pogo. | said asked
12. Zing _____, 'I can't hear you – my music is too loud!' | commented yelled

Easy! Have a musical sticker.

Colour in your score.

Silent letters

Ssshh! I wish people would be a little quieter! Can't they see I'm trying to sleep? Thankfully, some words contain letters that are completely **silent**.

knife   thum**b**   **w**rite

Words with silent letters can be tricky to spell, but at least they let sleeping dogs lie!

Circle the silent letters in these words.

1.  half
2.  where
3.  sword
4.  knee
5.  wrist
6.  honest

7.  should
8.  lamb
9. 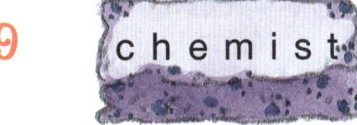 chemist
10.  folk
11.  debt
12.  gnome

 Good work! Have a Z cookie sticker.

Colour in your score.

TEST 13 Compound words

I love bouncing about, but sometimes I have accidents and things get broken. I've just ruined Nok's football. Oops! **Football** is a **compound word**, which means it's made of two words fixed together.

foot   ball

Knowing which words a compound word contains can make it easier to spell.

Ready, steady, bounce!

Match up each word with one from the bags to make a compound word.

1 note
2 hair
3 hand
4 cup
5 candle
6 arm
7 book
8 sauce
9 door
10 neck
11 lunch
12 lamp

Bags: stick, board, shade, pan, brush, chair, bag, book, knob, box, lace, case

Put a spring in your step! Have a springy sticker.

Colour in your score.

Test 14: Suffixes ly and ful

Err, what? **Suffixes** really tangle my antennae! The suffixes **ly** and **ful** go at the end of some words and change their meaning to help you describe what things are like, or how they are done.

love**ly**   hope**ful**

But how do you know which one to use? I guess you just have to try which one sounds right!

Some of these word sums make real words and some do not. Put a tick beside the ones you think make real words.

1. beauty + ly ☐
2. quick + ly ☐
3. sad + ful ☐
4. glad + ly ☐
5. slow + ful ☐
6. sorrow + ly ☐
7. hope + ful ☐
8. shame + ly ☐
9. joy + ful ☐
10. power + ful ☐
11. play + ly ☐
12. brave + ly ☐

Goal! Have a football sticker.

Colour in your score.

Contracting words

Mini T goes everywhere with me! Sometimes pairs of words are used together so often that we take out a letter or two, pop in an apostrophe and join them together. Don't you think that's clever, Mini T?

do not → don't   she will → she'll

Have you noticed that contracted words sound more like how we speak? Hurray!

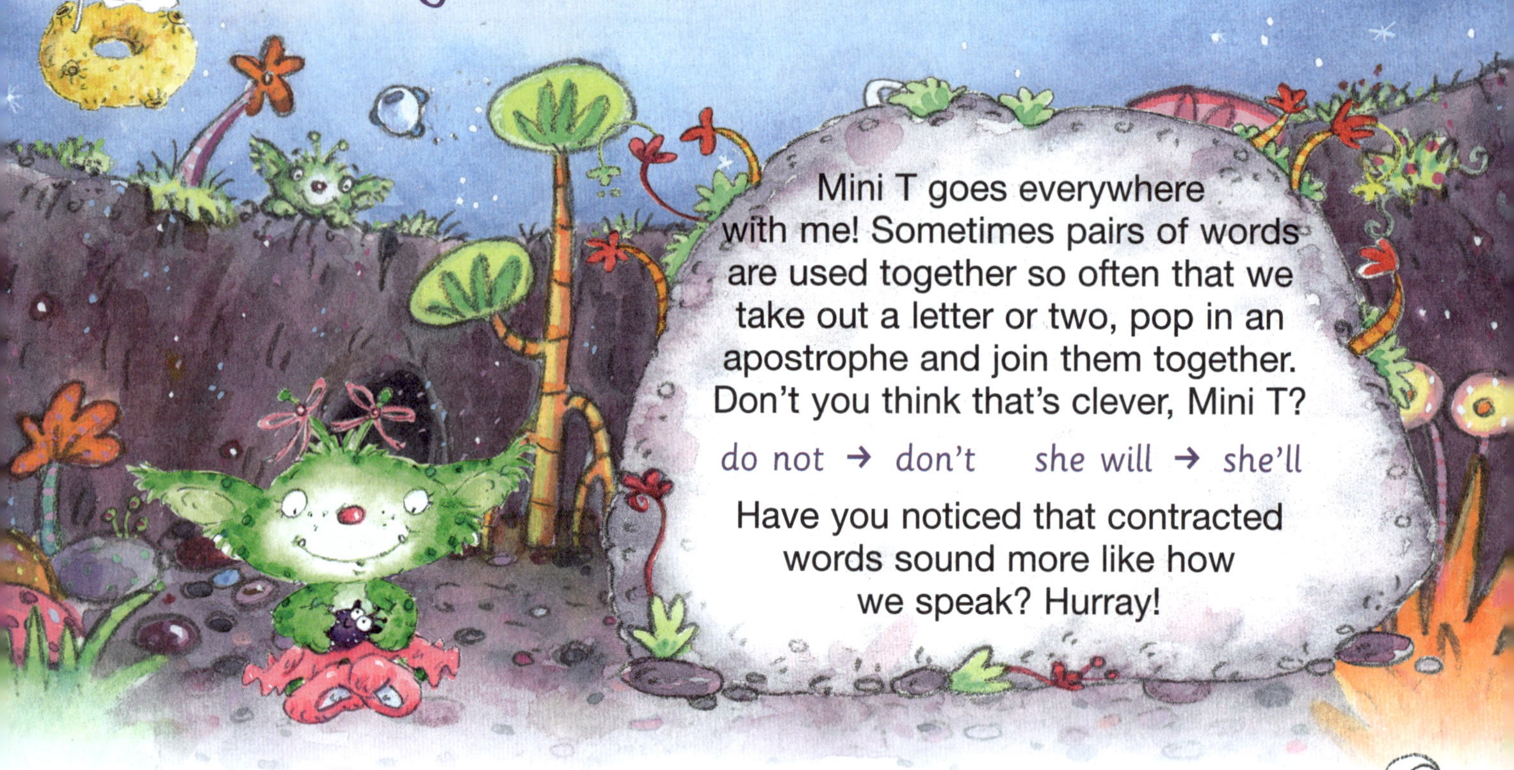

Write down the contracted forms of these pairs of words.

1   can not   _____
2   he would   _____
3   we will   _____
4   they have   _____
5   should not _____
6   I have   _____
7   she is   _____
8   I am   _____
9   have not   _____
10 it is   _____
11 is not   _____
12 will not   _____

Hurray! Have a Mini T sticker.

Colour in your score.

Prefixes mis and non

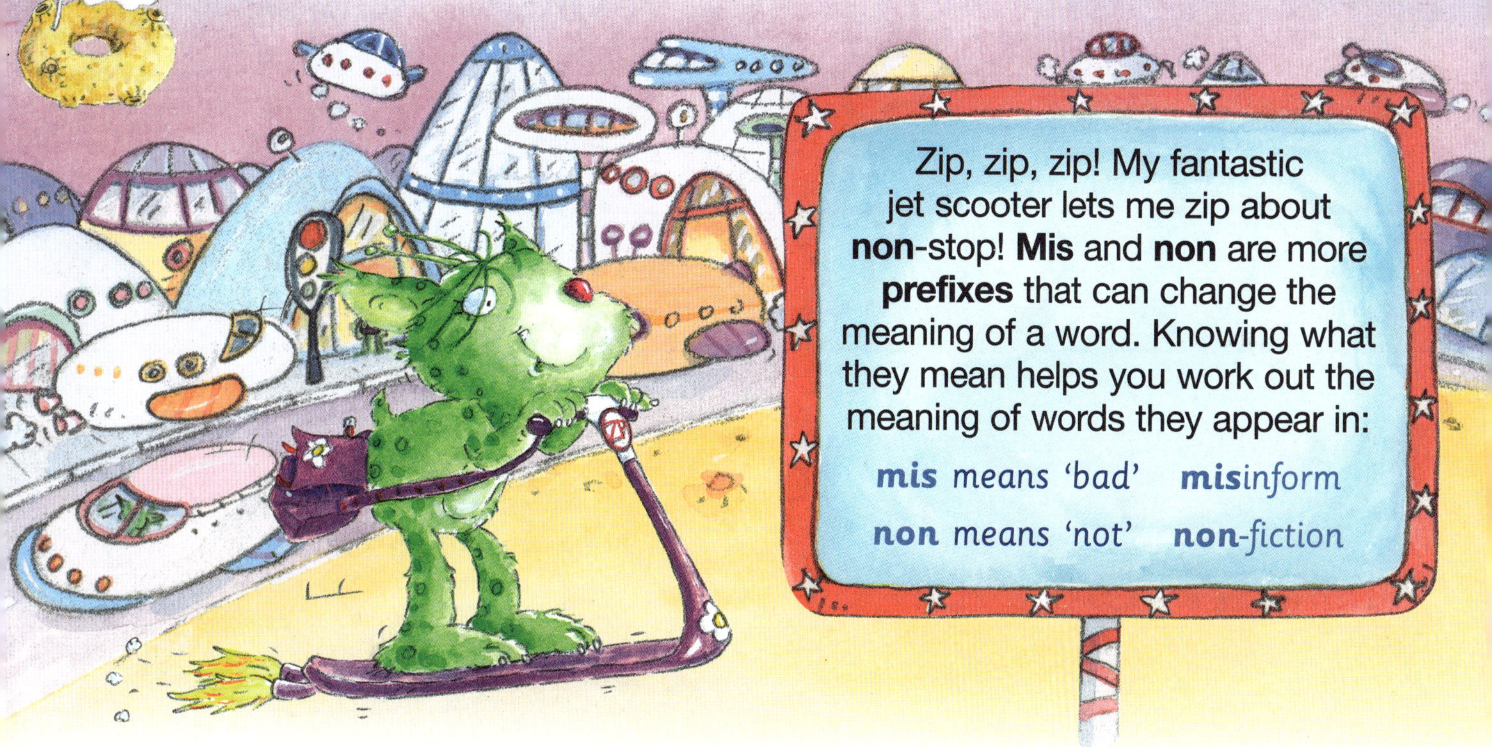

Zip, zip, zip! My fantastic jet scooter lets me zip about **non**-stop! **Mis** and **non** are more **prefixes** that can change the meaning of a word. Knowing what they mean helps you work out the meaning of words they appear in:
mis means 'bad' **mis**inform
non means 'not' **non**-fiction

Fill in the missing prefix. Just choose mis and non to add to each of these words.

1 ________take

2 ________toxic

3 ________sense

4 ________print

5 ________lead

6 ________treat

7 ________understand

8 ________existent

9 ________trust

10 ________stick

11 ________place

12 ________stop

12
11
10
9
8
7
6
5
4
3
2
1

Colour in your score.

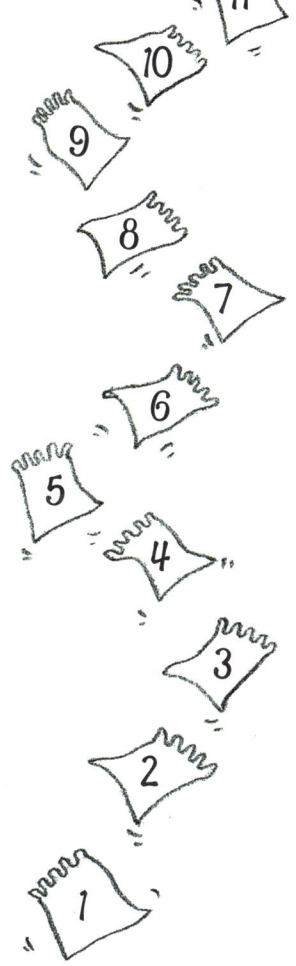

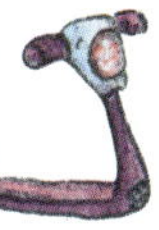

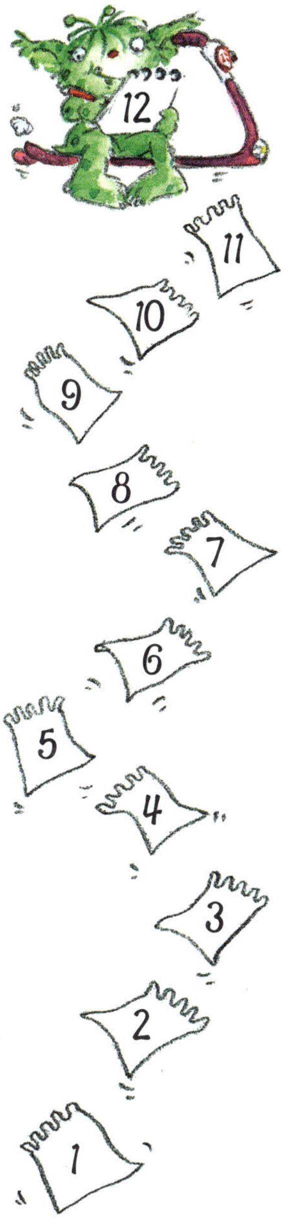

You're zippy! Have a scooter sticker.

Test 17 — Antonyms

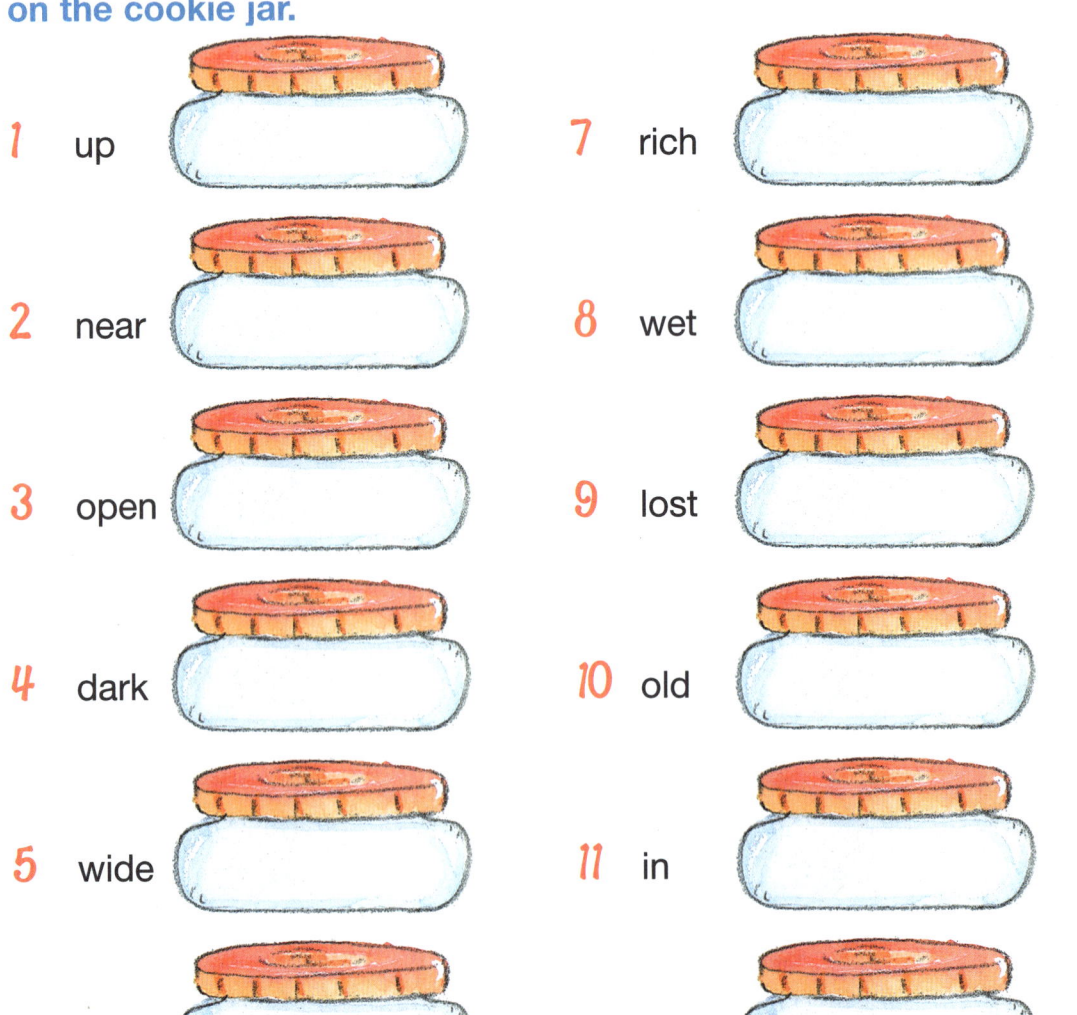

My tummy was full before, but now it's empty again.

full   empty

Full and empty are **antonyms** – or opposites. Antonyms can help us to compare things in our writing. Just like these biscuits can make my tummy full again!

Think of an antonym for each of these words. Write your answer on the cookie jar.

1 up
2 near
3 open
4 dark
5 wide
6 soft
7 rich
8 wet
9 lost
10 old
11 in
12 late

 Good work! Have a Z cookie sticker.

Colour in your score.

Adjectives

It's a **fantastic** day for just relaxing and enjoying the **beautiful** planet of Dunk.

Adjectives like fantastic and beautiful can help you describe people or things. If you choose them carefully, they'll help your reader to imagine what people, places and things are like, a bit like painting a picture. Cool!

Underline the adjective in each sentence.

1. It is cold in space.
2. The Moon is very bright.
3. Twinx is wearing red ribbons.
4. Nok is great at football.
5. Pogo is so funny!
6. Planet Dunk is brilliant!
7. Is Zen hungry again?
8. Zara P is clever.
9. Zing's music is too loud.
10. Twinx wears pink ballet slippers.
11. The craters on planet Dunk are round.
12. Twinx's Mini T is tiny.

Easy! Have a musical sticker.

Colour in your score.

Test 19: Homonyms

> Do you think Zen is asleep or awake? It's hard to tell just by looking! **Homonyms** are a bit like that too. They are words which look the same, but have different meanings. 
>
> wave   wave
>
> Because they are spelt exactly the same, you have to look at the whole sentence to be sure of the meaning.

Circle the word in each pair that has a homonym.

1. hat / tap
2. hot / bat
3. ball / roof
4. door / ring
5. form / car
6. wall / firm
7. sun / rose
8. watch / vase
9. sofa / spring
10. book / nose
11. sky / saw
12. band / wand

 Put a spring in your step! Have a springy sticker.

Colour in your score.

Test 20 Pronouns

Did you know that you can sometimes use personal **pronouns** like **I**, **you**, **him**, **her** and **they**, instead of proper nouns, like people's names?

Nok and Zing play football. They kick the ball between them.

They save you from having to use the same names again and again. Hurray!

Choose the best personal pronoun to complete each sentence.

1 Mini T is my friend and I love _____. me / her
2 Pogo and Zen are always together, because _____ are best friends. we / they
3 'Shall _____ dance?' Twinx asked Mini T. you / we
4 Pogo and Zen have left _____ cookies behind. their / her
5 Zara P is on her jet scooter. Can you see _____? him / her
6 Nok complained, '_____ can't find my baseball cap.' us / I
7 'Where are Pogo and Zen? I can't find _____,' said Twinx. us / them
8 'Wait for _____!' shouted Zing and Pogo. he / us
9 There is Zing. Is _____ listening to music again? she / he
10 Pogo gives Zen Z cookies to wake _____ up. him / them
11 'Pass _____ the ball!' yelled Nok. us / me
12 Zara P remembers interesting things, then _____ writes them in her notebook. she / we

Hurray! Have a Mini T sticker.

Colour in your score.

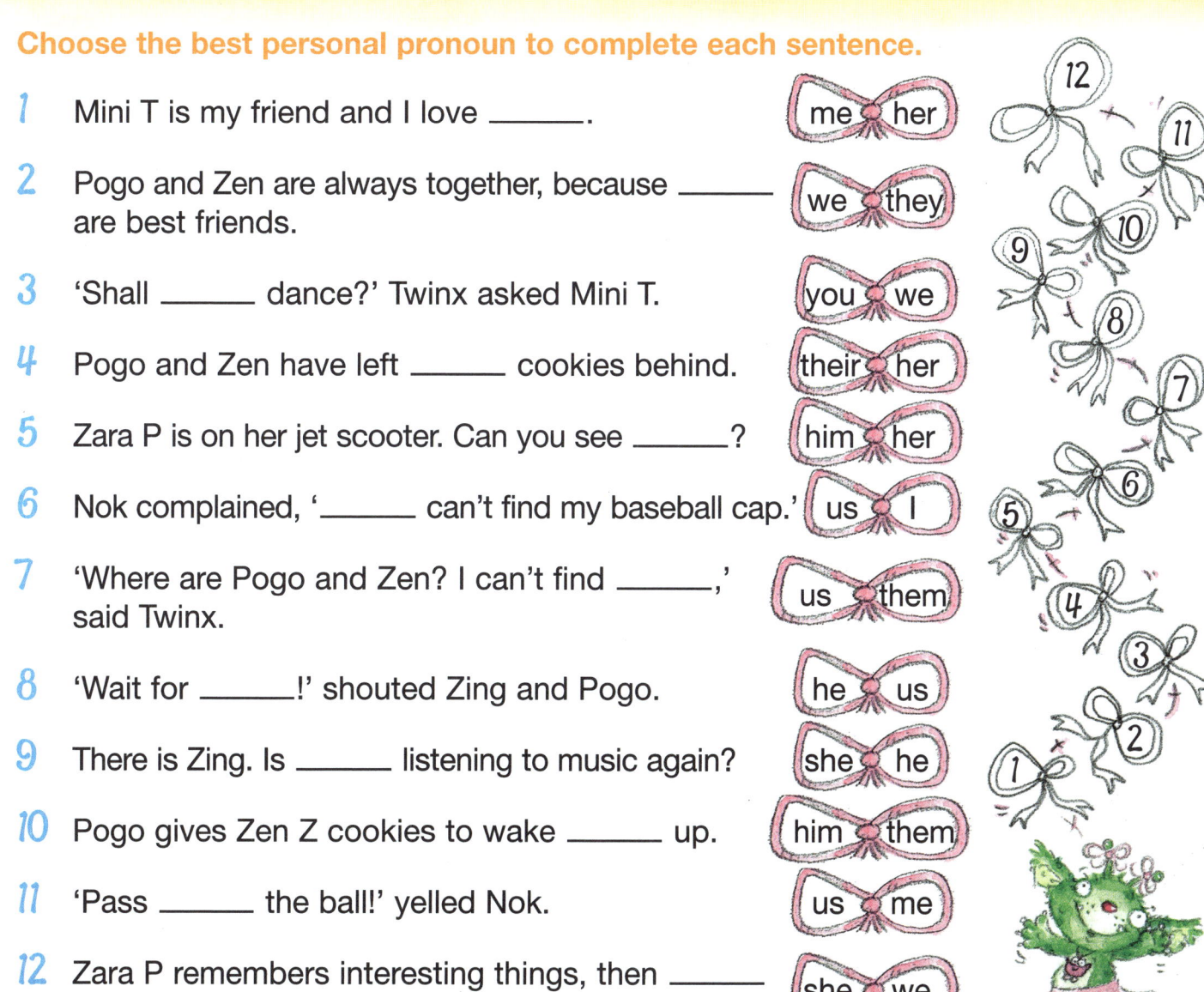

Conjunctions

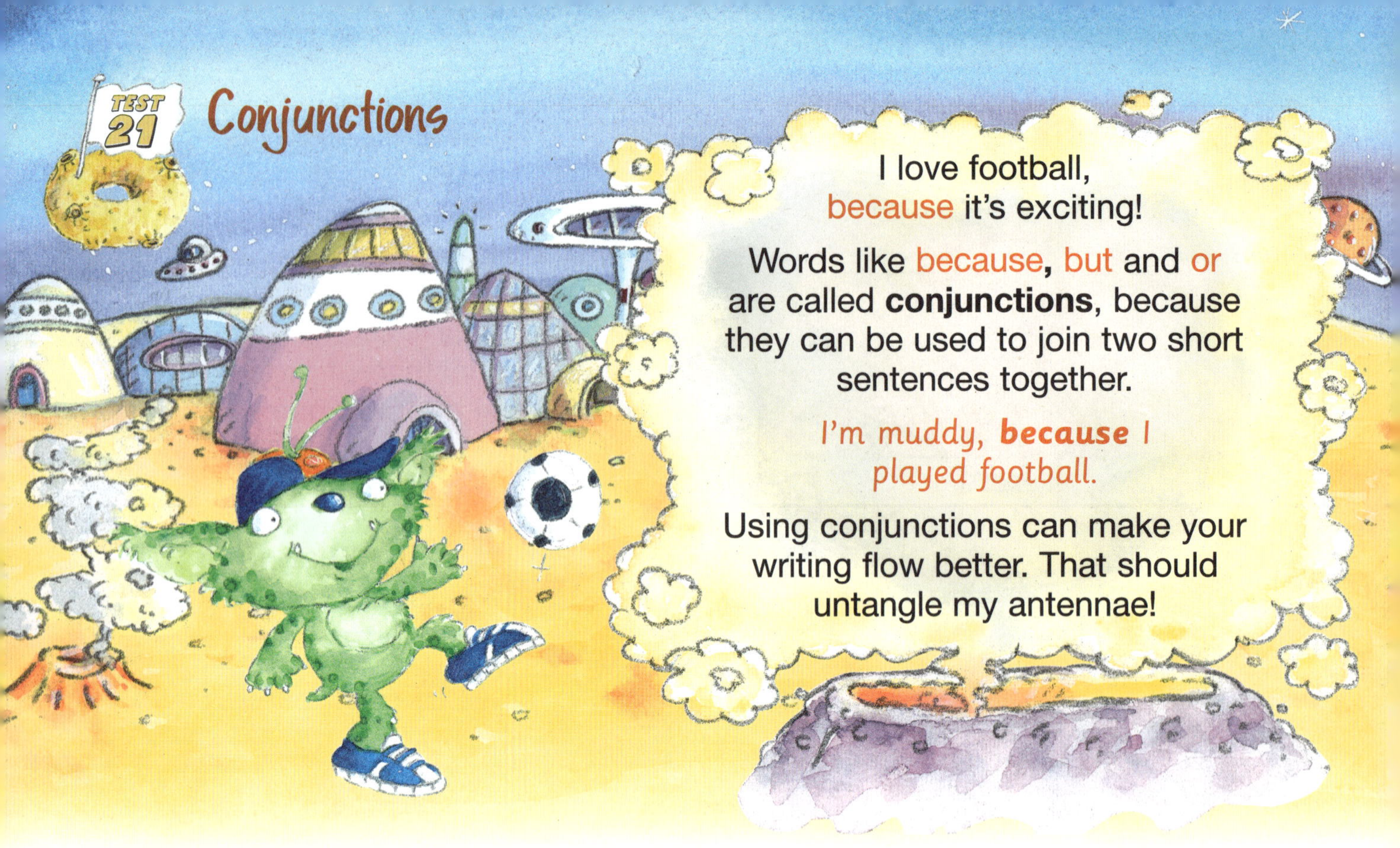

I love football, **because** it's exciting!

Words like **because**, **but** and **or** are called **conjunctions**, because they can be used to join two short sentences together.

I'm muddy, **because** I played football.

Using conjunctions can make your writing flow better. That should untangle my antennae!

Underline the conjunctions in these sentences.

1 Zen wanted a cookie, but they had all gone.

2 Zara P carries a notebook, so she can make notes.

3 Twinx wears pink, because it is her favourite colour.

4 The aliens must wait while the space-mobile is being refuelled.

5 Pogo can bounce, because he has springs on his trainers.

6 Zen might have some Z cookies, or he might have a nap.

7 The aliens came to planet Earth after they won a competition.

8 Twinx wears her ballet shoes when she is dancing.

9 Earthlings cannot visit planet Dunk, as it is too far away.

10 Pogo gives Zen a Z cookie, if he is hungry.

11 Zara P hopped on her jet scooter, but it would not start.

12 Zen was asleep, when Pogo bounced past.

Goal! Have a football sticker.

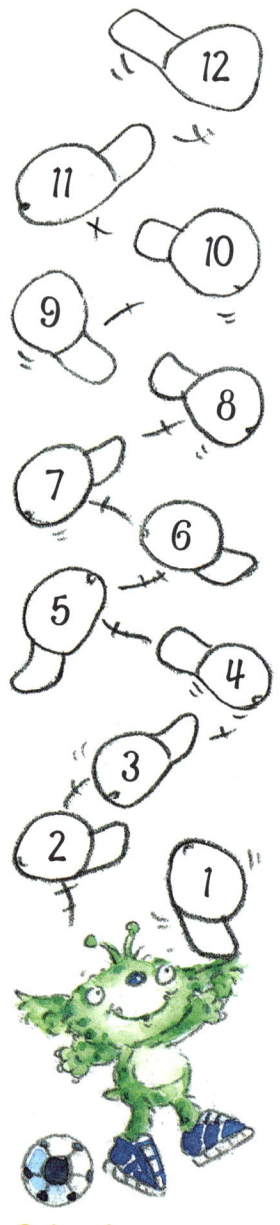
Colour in your score.

TEST 22 Commas

Yawn! I don't need any encouragement to take a break, unlike Pogo, who never stops! His writing is just the same too. He should learn to use **commas**, to tell his readers when to pause.

I ate my Z cookies, then had a nap.

See? So simple I could do it in my... zzz!

Add the commas to these sentences. Read them out loud to help

1 Zing the oldest in the Alien Club is really cool.

2 Don't worry Zara P will help you.

3 After tea Nok always plays football.

4 Eventually Zen fell asleep.

5 Nok's antennae got tangled because he was confused.

6 On her jet scooter Zara P is the fastest alien.

7 Twinx loves to dance listening to music.

8 Pogo's rucksack on his back is full of Z cookies.

9 Zing's music is so loud you can hear him light years away.

10 Twinx loves pretty frilly things.

11 With a huge leap Pogo bounced right over the crater.

12 Yesterday after his nap Zen ate a whole box of Z cookies.

Good work! Have a Z cookie sticker.

Colour in your score.

Test 23 — Nouns

Boing, boing, boing! I can see all sorts of things from up here – craters, stars, planets... **Nouns** are words that name things, like craters, stars and planets! They are special because only nouns can be singular or plural.

Some nouns have plurals, like moons.

Some nouns don't, like astral rain.

Sort these words into the correct planet, depending on whether they are singular, plural, or have no plural form.

1. picture
2. mice
3. space-mobile
4. sunshine
5. worries
6. book
7. milk
8. trees
9. hay
10. children
11. thunder
12. cow

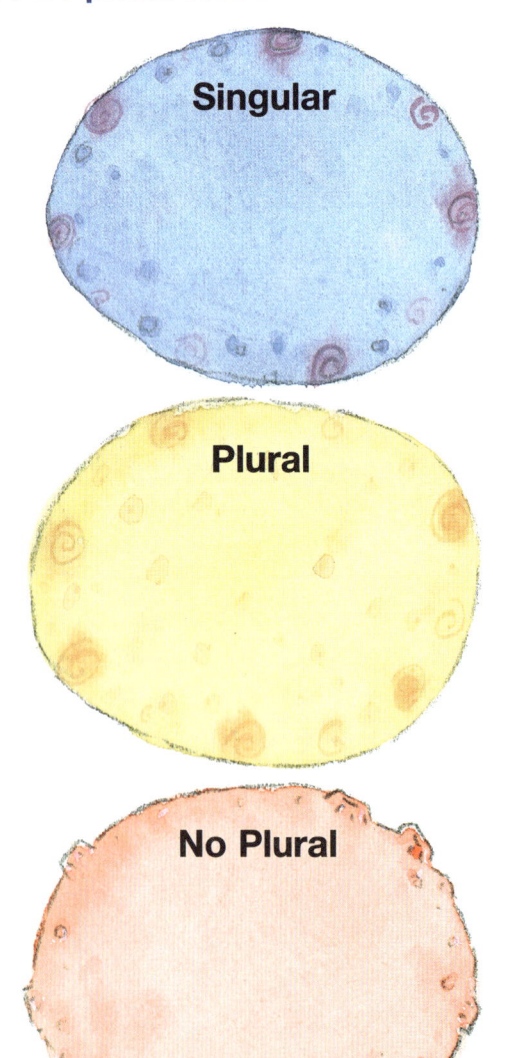

Singular

Plural

No Plural

Put a spring in your step! Have a springy sticker.

Colour in your score.

Fact and fiction

I was just having a wonderful dream.

If only my dream was **fact**, not **fiction**! If something is fact, it's true. Fact is sometimes called non-fiction too. Fiction is made up, although some fictional stories are based on real people, places or events.

I could do with a Z cookie now, and that's a fact!

Read each sentence and decide whether you think each one is fact or fiction. If it's fiction, draw a dream cloud round it, like this –

1. Dragons really exist.
2. London is the capital city of England.
3. There are fairies at the bottom of my garden.
4. Jack really did climb a huge beanstalk.
5. Africa is a continent.
6. Squares have four sides.
7. Cats really do have nine lives.
8. Mixing white and red makes pink.
9. Apples grow on trees.
10. Goldilocks ate the three bears' porridge.
11. Witches fly on broomsticks.
12. Man has walked on the Moon.

Good work! Have a Z cookie sticker.

Colour in your score.

Test 25 — Instructions

My notebook contains all sorts of information. There are recipes, lists of rules, timetables, notes on how to make things and how to get to places.

They are all types of **instructions**, because they help me to do something the right way. Instructions have to be set out clearly, to make them easy to understand.

Draw lines to join each page heading to the correct description.

1. Jet scooter racing: the rules
2. Directions to space-mobile port
3. Space-mobile schedule
4. Cheese Omelettes
5. How to build an anti-gravity belt
6. Dunk TV Times, Friday
7. Jet scooter engine repairs
8. Football: the offside rule
9. Quick meals: potato fritters
10. Space-mobile route to planet Earth
11. Strawberry Smoothie
12. Orion Cinema: how to find us

- recipes
- rules
- directions
- construction instructions
- timetables

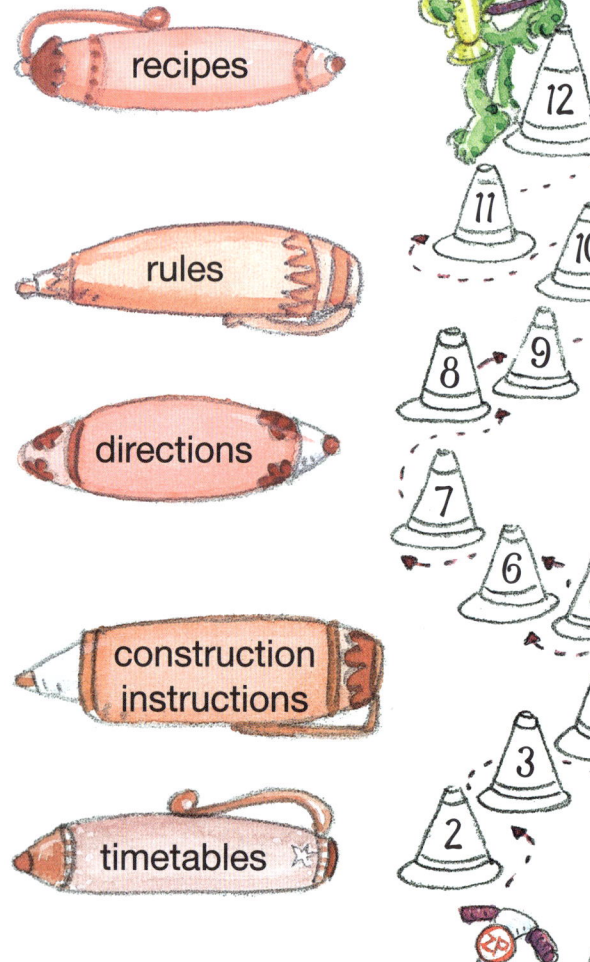

Zip, zip, zip! Have a scooter sticker.

Colour in your score.

TEST 26

Words within words

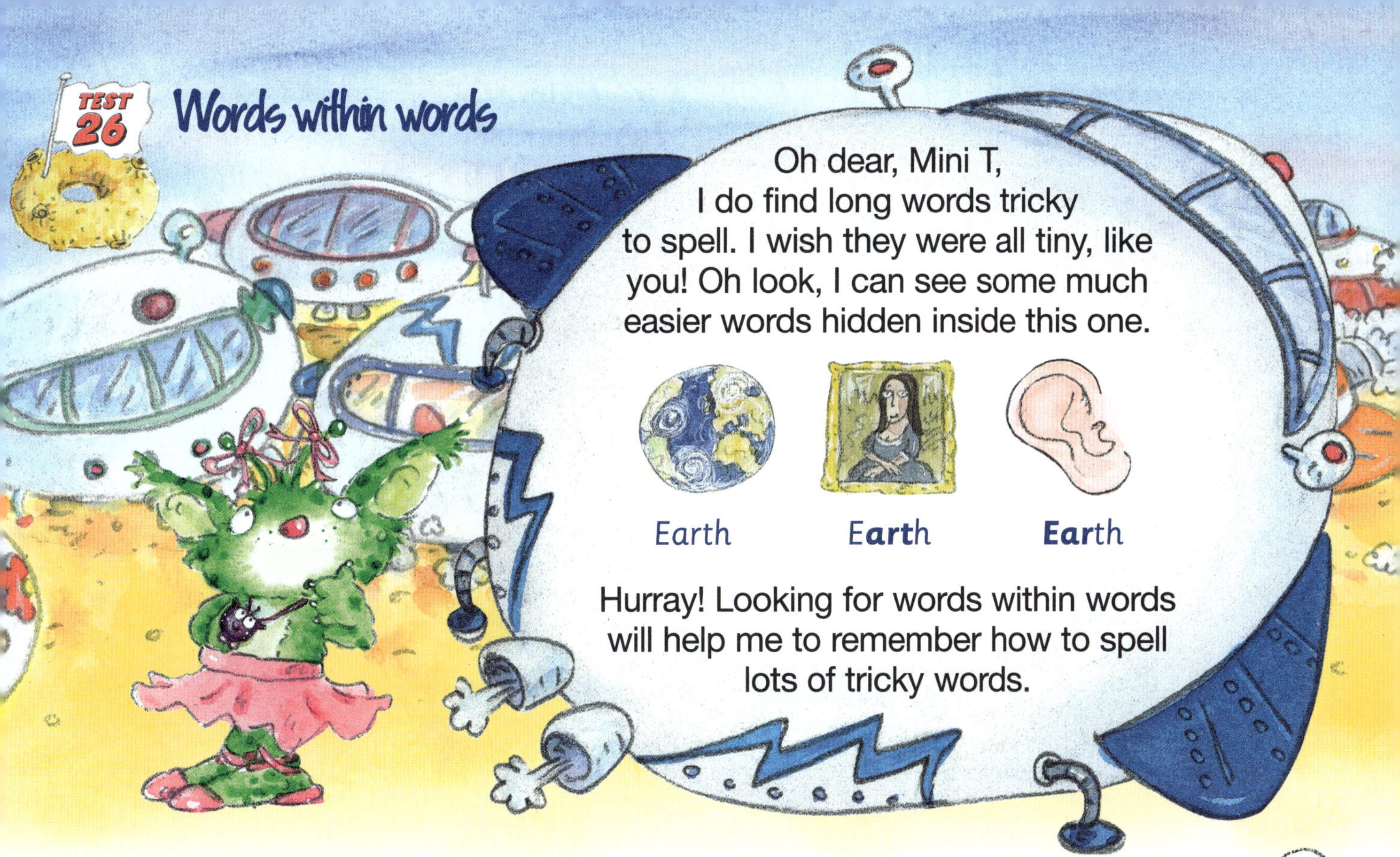

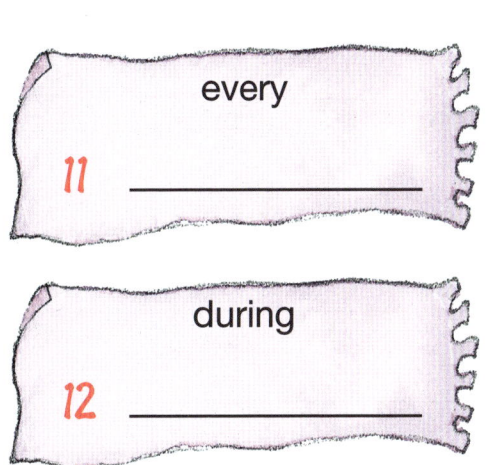

Oh dear, Mini T,
I do find long words tricky to spell. I wish they were all tiny, like you! Oh look, I can see some much easier words hidden inside this one.
Earth
E**arth**
Earth
Hurray! Looking for words within words will help me to remember how to spell lots of tricky words.

Find the easy words hiding inside these longer ones. Look carefully, though, as some words have more than one!

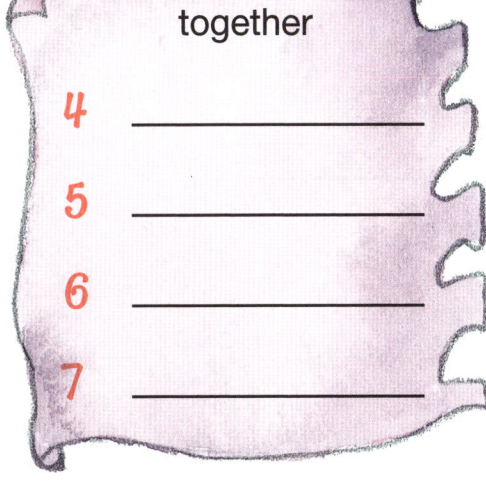

important

1 ____________

2 ____________

3 ____________

together

4 ____________

5 ____________

6 ____________

7 ____________

heard

8 ____________

9 ____________

young

10 ____________

every

11 ____________

during

12 ____________

12
11
10
9
8
7
6
5
4
3
2
1

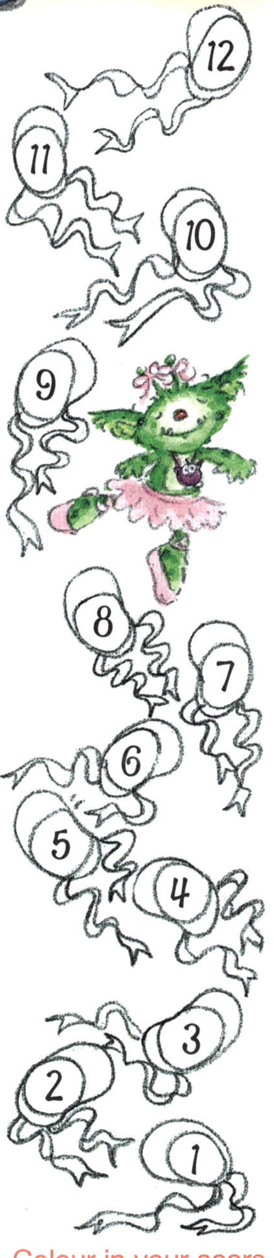

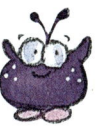

Hurray! Have a Mini T sticker.

Colour in your score.

TEST 27 Setting

Zen isn't fussy about where he eats or sleeps. He'll do it anywhere! In stories, though, the places where things happen can be very important. A well-described **setting** can really help your readers imagine what's going on. Use lots of adjectives to paint a picture!

Zen sank into a pile of plump cushions arranged on a red velvet sofa.

What do you think planet Dunk looks like? Think of some great descriptions to complete these sentences.

1 From space, Dunk looks like a _____.

2 The colour of the sky around the planet is _____.

3 The weather is _____.

4 The craters are _____.

5 Small boats float on _____ lakes.

6 Aliens live in houses that look like _____.

7 From their windows, you can see fine views of _____.

8 Outside, their gardens _____.

9 People travel about in _____.

10 They buy _____ from shops in the cities.

11 They watch films in _____ cinemas.

12 They play _____ on huge, floodlit pitches.

Put a spring in your step! Have a springy sticker.

Colour in your score.

TEST 28: Finding information

I'm reading a book about some of my favourite bands. It's amazing! As with most non-fiction books, the pages are numbered and a contents page at the front tells you what page each chapter or section starts on. Even better, the index at the back lists all the topics alphabetically, with their page numbers. Then headings on the pages help you find what you're looking for. Cool!

Put true (T) or false (F) beside each of these statements about finding information in non-fiction books.

1. Non-fiction books are organised to make it easy to find the information you need.
2. The contents page is at the back of a book.
3. The pages of most non-fiction books are numbered.
4. The index is at the front of the book.
5. Non-fiction books often organise information into chapters or sections.
6. Indexes are arranged in page order.
7. The contents page tells you what page each chapter starts on.
8. Headings on the pages tell you where to look in the index.
9. You have to read all of a non-fiction book to find the information you need.
10. Indexes are arranged in alphabetical order.
11. Headings help you to find information on the page.
12. The contents page is at the front of a book.

Congratulations! Have a last musical sticker for your certificate. Cool!

Colour in your score.

Answers

Test 1 Adding ing
1. running
2. making
3. raining
4. tapping
5. playing
6. going
7. swimming
8. taking
9. hoping
10. dancing
11. saying
12. winning

Test 2 le endings
Correctly spelt and circled words are:
1. apple
2. bottle
3. petal
4. angel
5. little
6. parcel
7. table
8. model
9. metal
10. pedal
11. medal
12. label

Test 3 The alphabet

A B E F H L M N O Q S T X Z

Test 4 Synonyms
1. scorching
2. hilarious
3. exhausted
4. miserable
5. gigantic
6. delighted
7. dazzling
8. starving
9. tiny
10. fascinating
11. smashed
12. ancient

Test 5 Handwriting
1. *paint pot*
2. *silver star*
3. *funny face*
4. *loud sound*
5. *grape vine*
6. *two twins*
7. *roundabout*
8. *full stop*
9. *table mat*
10. *fairground*
11. *white cloud*
12. *wild witch*

Test 6 Verbs
1. sprint
2. scrub
3. locate
4. consume
5. notice
6. stroll
7. chat
8. conceal
9. doze
10. shatter
11. construct
12. giggle

Test 7 Prefixes
1. not done
2. before school
3. vanish, not appear
4. not usual
5. not approve
6. not pleased
7. not dressed
8. paint again
9. cooked before, already cooked
10. write again
11. form again
12. paid before or already paid

Test 8 Verb tenses
1. walked
2. buy
3. saved
4. tipped
5. hide
6. write
7. hurried
8. swam
9. run
10. grew
11. see
12. know

Test 9 Speech marks
1. 'I'm playing football later,' said Nok.
2. Zing said, 'This music is so cool.'
3. 'Can I have a Z cookie?' asked Zen.
4. Zara P said, 'Do you like my scooter?'
5. Twinx said, 'I'm dancing with Mini T.'
6. Pogo said, 'Just bouncing around!'
7. Nok shouted, 'Did you see that goal?'
8. Zen mumbled, 'I'm sleepy.'
9. 'Look at my new music player,' said Zing.
10. 'Here comes the space-mobile,' said Zara P.
11. Pogo said, 'Let's hop over to the crater field.'
12. Twinx asked, 'Do you like my dance?'

Test 10 er and est
1. tallest
2. hungry
3. shorter
4. closest
5. dark
6. prettiest
7. happy
8. late
9. safest
10. hot
11. fitter
12. older

Test 11 Writing dialogue
Circled words should be:
1. shouted
2. yawned
3. asked
4. replied
5. demanded
6. explained
7. warned
8. advised
9. observed
10. grumbled
11. asked
12. yelled

Test 12 Silent letters
1. h a (l) f
2. w (h) e r e
3. s (w) o r d
4. (k) n e e
5. (w) r i s t
6. (h) o n e s t
7. s h o u (l) d
8. l a m (b)
9. c (h) e m i s t
10. f o (l) k
11. d e (b) t
12. (g) n o m e

Test 13 Compound words
1. notebook
2. hairbrush
3. handbag
4. cupboard
5. candlestick
6. armchair
7. bookcase
8. saucepan
9. doorknob
10. necklace
11. lunchbox
12. lampshade

Test 14 Suffixes ly and ful
The real words are:
2. quickly
4. gladly
7. hopeful
9. joyful
10. powerful
12. bravely

Test 15 Contracting words
1. can't
2. he'd
3. we'll
4. they've
5. shouldn't
6. I've
7. she's
8. I'm
9. haven't
10. it's
11. isn't
12. won't

Test 16 Prefixes mis and non
1. mistake
2. non-toxic
3. nonsense
4. misprint
5. mislead
6. mistreat
7. misunderstand
8. non-existent
9. mistrust
10. non-stick
11. misplace
12. non-stop

Test 17 Antonyms
Several answers are possible, but good answers may include:
1. down
2. far
3. close, shut
4. light
5. narrow
6. hard
7. poor
8. dry
9. found
10. young, new
11. out
12. early

Test 18 Adjectives
1. It is <u>cold</u> in space.
2. The Moon is very <u>bright</u>.
3. Twinx is wearing <u>red</u> ribbons.
4. Nok is <u>great</u> at football.
5. Pogo is so <u>funny</u>!
6. Planet Dunk is <u>brilliant</u>!
7. Is Zen <u>hungry</u> again?
8. Zara P is <u>clever</u>.
9. Zing's music is too <u>loud</u>.
10. Twinx wears <u>pink</u> ballet slippers.
11. The craters on planet Dunk are <u>round</u>.
12. Twinx's Mini T is <u>tiny</u>.

Test 19 Homonyms
1. tap
2. bat
3. ball
4. ring
5. form
6. firm
7. rose
8. watch
9. spring
10. book
11. saw
12. band

Test 20 Pronouns
1. her
2. they
3. we
4. their
5. her
6. I
7. them
8. us
9. he
10. him
11. me
12. she

Test 21 Conjunctions
1. Zen wanted a cookie, <u>but</u> they had all gone.
2. Zara P carries a notebook, <u>so</u> she can make notes.
3. Twinx wears pink, <u>because</u> it is her favourite colour.
4. The aliens must wait <u>while</u> the space-mobile is being refuelled.
5. Pogo can bounce, <u>because</u> he has springs on his trainers.
6. Zen might have some Z cookies, <u>or</u> he might have a nap.
7. The aliens came to planet Earth <u>after</u> they won a competition.
8. Twinx wears her ballet shoes <u>when</u> she is dancing.
9. Earthlings cannot visit planet Dunk, <u>as</u> it is too far away.
10. Pogo gives Zen a Z cookie, <u>if</u> he is hungry.
11. Zara P hopped on her jet scooter, <u>but</u> it would not start.
12. Zen was asleep, <u>when</u> Pogo bounced past.

Test 22 Commas
1. Zing, the oldest in the Alien Club, is really cool.
2. Don't worry, Zara P will help you.
3. After tea, Nok always plays football.
4. Eventually, Zen fell asleep.
5. Nok's antennae got tangled, because he was confused.
6. On her jet scooter, Zara P is the fastest alien.
7. Twinx loves to dance, listening to music.
8. Pogo's rucksack, on his back, is full of Z cookies.
9. Zing's music is so loud, you can hear him light years away.
10. Twinx loves pretty, frilly things.
11. With a huge leap, Pogo bounced right over the crater.
12. Yesterday, after his nap, Zen ate a whole box of Z cookies.

Test 23 Nouns
Singular nouns: picture, space-mobile, book, cow
Plural nouns: mice, worries, trees, children
Nouns with no plural form: sunshine, milk, hay, thunder

Test 24 Fact and fiction
Fictional sentences are: **1**, **3**, **4**, **7**, **10** and **11**.

Test 25 Instructions
Recipes:
Cheese Omelettes
Quick meals: potato fritters
Strawberry Smoothie

Rules:
Jet scooter racing: the rules
Football: the offside rule

Directions:
Directions to space-mobile port
Space-mobile route to planet Earth
Orion Cinema: how to find us

Construction instructions:
How to build an anti-gravity belt
Jet scooter engine repairs

Timetables:
Space-mobile schedule
Dunk TV Times, Friday

Test 26 Words within words
Any of the following are possible:
1–3 imp, port, or, ant, import, an
4–7 to, get, her, the
8–9 ear, he, hear
10 you
11 very, ever
12 ring, in

Test 27 Setting
Many answers are possible, but strong answers will contain lots of descriptive adjectives and adverbs.

Test 28 Finding information
1. T
2. F
3. T
4. F
5. T
6. F
7. T
8. F
9. F
10. T
11. T
12. T

Alien Club Certificate

Congratulations, _____, from everyone on planet Dunk!
You have collected all your award stickers and are now a member of the
English 7-8 Alien Club.
You are out of this world!